EXPLORING OUNDLE

AND

SURROUNDING VILLAGES

A tour of Oundle and villages within a six mile radius of the town.

by

Ian Bishop

Jema Publications

Published 1995 by Jema Publications

ISBN 1-871468-23-X

Publishers' Note
Every care has been taken in the preparation of this book and all the information has been carefully checked and is believed to be correct at the time of publication. However, neither the author nor the publishers can accept responsibility for any errors or omissions or for any loss, damage, injury or inconvenience resulting from the use of this book.

Jema Publications
40 Ashley Lane
Moulton
Northampton
NN3 7TJ

Printed in Great Britain by Woolnough Bookbinding Ltd., Wellingborough

CONTENTS

INTRODUCTION

After several years in East Northamptonshire it came forcibly to my attention that although Oundle and the villages around were well-loved, very little was available specifically about the area.

In deciding what to include I opted for a roughly six-mile (10km) circle around the town centre which splits neatly into three segments bounded by the A427 to the west and the A605 running southwest - northeast. As a result exploration for the road user can be easily arranged, whilst for the walker or horse-person there are a wealth of public footpaths, bridleways and minor roads extending over the entire area. To assist in planning I have provided a list of cross-country footpaths from each location.

The idea behind this guide is to put some flesh on the bare bones of what the traveller may see on his or her journeying. It has not been my intention to produce a history of Oundle or the villages as there are others better qualified to do that, but historical notes have been included where they will enhance the knowledge of the visual.

The topography of the area is of gently rising land running east to west, with the underlying strata a complex mixture of limestone, sand, gravel and cornbrash. Gravel extraction has been and continues to be an important source of employment. Meandering across the landscape is the River Nene and southern parts of the area contain pockets of the once immense Rockingham Forest.

In 655AD Peada, King of Mercia founded a monastery at Medehampstead (Peterborough) as a mission station, known then as a Minster, to convert the peoples of South Mercia from their animist religions to Christianity. Consequently today the dominant feature in almost every village are the churches which have been built as a response to that. Sadly, some have to be kept locked, but keys are often obtainable from local houses.

If readily available I have included some details of churches and other buildings, to whet the explorer's appetite. There is often further historical information to be had in the places themselves and in other books of local interest. (See Bibliography).

I urge wanderers to get hold of these for themselves and the Ordnance Survey Landranger maps Nos 141 and 142 which cover the area. I have also included notes on inns and public houses, landmarks and other structures or items of interest where possible.

The book is divided into four sections; Oundle; villages to the north and west; those to the south-west and the largest area, to the east. A list of the villages covered is included at the start of each section and in the index. Also given is a grid reference for each place, (normally the parish church) and where known, the population from the 1991 census.

Visitors to Oundle should be aware that Oundle School and the footpaths surrounding it (except St. Peter's churchyard) are private property with no rights of way.

I shall not be surprised if the book contains errors and omissions; there are often contradictions which cannot be easily resolved when compiling a guide. Any opinions expressed are my own and I take responsibility for them.

My special thanks go to Tony Noble for helping a dream become a reality and to Geoff Cameron who laboured through the original manuscript and offered helpful suggestions. Also to the many friends who, sometimes unwittingly, contributed snippets of local history and interest. Not least thanks to my wife, Kathryn, who gave me the encouragement and spent happy hours with me in researching facts.

Ian Bishop
February 1995

OUNDLE

TL042883 ***Population 3996***

At the centre of this circle of exploration the town has developed at a giant horseshoe bend on the River Nene. The occupying Roman forces built a road the course of which is now followed in part by the A605, but the site is much older, with references to a monastery founded by St. Wilfrid, Abbot of Ripton and Bishop of York, possibly on the site of the present parish church, in the late 7th century when the settlement seems to have been known as Undolum.

In the Middle Ages the town was the lowest crossing point of the Nene and the river was navigable up to Oundle from 1730. Consequently it became an important trading post with river wharves. Another large trade was that of brewing and malting and there are traces of this all over the town.

Present day travellers find a town of about 4,000 people (plus about 800 boarders at the town's public school in term time) offering a variety of goods and services to residents and visitors alike. There are three public car parks, that behind the supermarket in St. Osyth's Lane has a two-hour limit, and there are public conveniences here; long-stay facilities are off East Road next to the District recycling centre and a third in Benefield Road adjacent to Oundle Museum.

Facilities include accountants, banks, a bookshop, butchers, a citizens advice bureau, clothing shops, a delicatessen, electrical goods, estate agents, gift shops, a greengrocer, a library, newsagents, pharmacies, restaurants, solicitors, supermarkets and a travel agent, together with other specialist retailers, plus a health centre, a dentist and an optician. There is a (part-time) police station, a fire-station manned by retained personnel and an ambulance is stationed in the town.

The town centre is attractive and well worth investigation on foot as there are many paths and alleyways between buildings. Of particular note are the many "Yards" such as Setchells, Turners or Danfords, with hidden cottages to the rear of West Street and North Street; or "Courts" like Crown Court off the Market Place. Some are private, others have footpaths through.

Oundle Market Place

A GUIDED TOUR OF THE TOWN

To explore the town, park in the long stay car park off East Road and walk through to the Market Place via East Road and St. Osyth's Lane. Note first, on the corner with St. Osyth's Lane, ***Bramston House [1],*** one of the boarding houses for Oundle School. This was originally the town house of Stephen Bramston, a lawyer, in the 18th century. It was bought by Oundle School in 1917 and enlarged to take in many adjoining premises.

The Tudor-style former ***Town Hall [2],*** at the centre of the Market Place dates from 1826 and carries on its south aspect the family crest of the Watts-Russell family, land owners in the district for many years.

Immediately to the north is the charming former ***town house [3],*** whose upper floors have been extended by the simple device of adding pillars at the front. It is now used as the chaplaincy to Oundle School and houses a fine Bookshop beneath which is open to the public. An open air market is held every Thursday and is marked by a bell rung at mid-day. Walk through the Bookshop Passage to reach the churchyard (of which more later), passing the School Library and Laxton School on your right.

In 1556 Sir William Laxton, a "local boy" and Lord Mayor of London, re-endowed the Oundle grammar school in his will and instructed that the old gild-house be acquired for the purpose. ***Laxton School [4],*** now stands on the site and is the day school for the non-boarders of Oundle School. Note inscriptions in Greek, Latin and Hebrew on a plate originally placed on the gild-house in 1593, together with a griffon on the roof pinnacle above the Cloisters entrance to the Laxton School. The present day Schoolroom is a 19th century copy of the original gild house.

St. Peter's Oundle

Laxton School was completed in the mid 1850's and its cloisters are the southern boundary to the churchyard of ***St. Peter's Parish Church [5],*** whereas the Oundle School cloisters form part of the western perimeter. From these origins eventually came the public school which now occupies over one quarter of the total land area of the town, either with buildings or playing fields. There are fourteen boarding houses around the town housing both boys and, since 1992, girls. The motto, "God Grant Grace" is carved onto each of the buildings which comprise the School.

Oundle School has been a vital part of the town for over four hundred years and each needs the other for both to succeed. The School provides diverse employment for

Guide To Town Trail

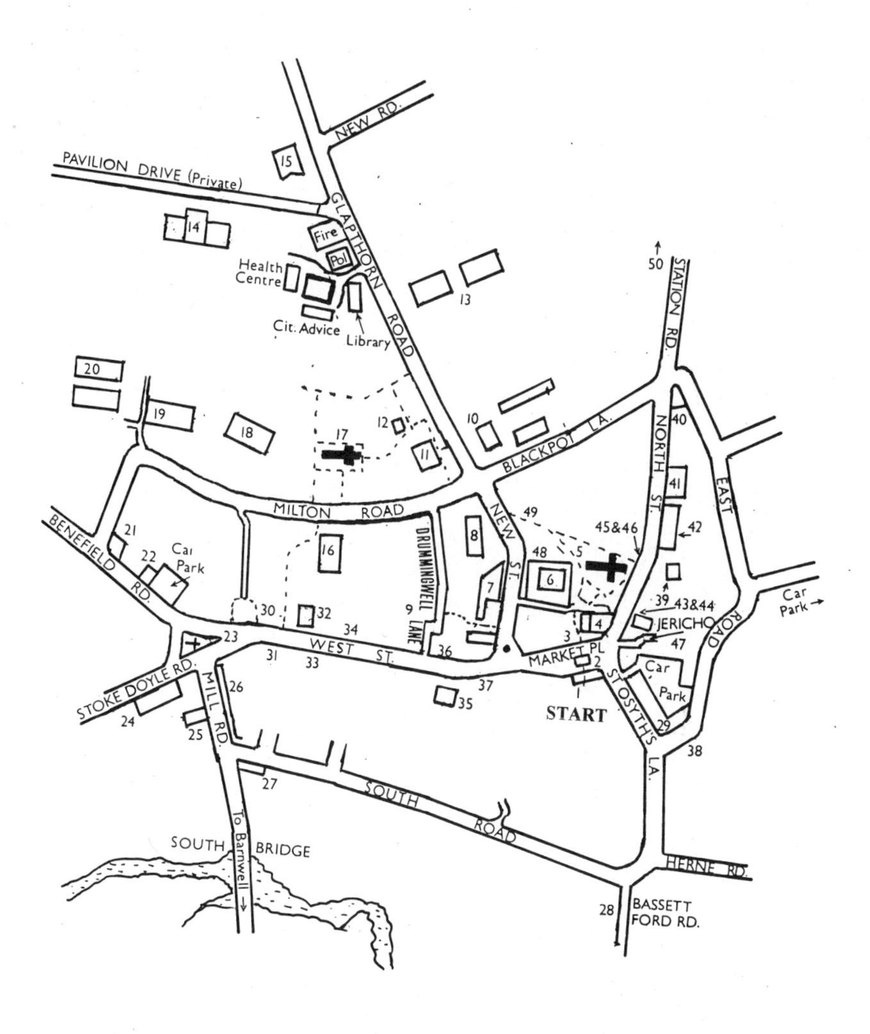

over 300 people thereby significantly prospering the local economy; in turn the area offers housing and various medical, social and retail activities and services in a pleasant rural aspect.

Next turn left into Church Street, with the ***Cloisters [6],*** (1881) on your right, on an inside wall of which is an engraved roll of boys on a foundation stone dated 1799, the oldest part. (Please note this is on private property.)

From here enter New Street: opposite is ***School House [7],*** (1887) with the adjacent Talbot Study Rooms behind an imposing gateway and lawns. To the right is the Great Hall, completed in the early 20th century. Left is the ***Talbot Inn [8],*** rebuilt in 1625 when it was known as the Tabret. The staircase is reputed to have come from the destroyed Fotheringhay Castle and the building has its share of local ghost stories.

Follow the pathway between the Inn's accomodation blocks to reach ***Drummingwell Lane [9],*** where the Methodist Church is located. In the 17th and 18th centuries the now defunct well was said to make a "drumming" sound and to foretell national disasters. Other Christian denominations meeting in the town include Quakers, Baptists and Roman Catholics, as well as Anglicans at St. Peter's.

Besides the Talbot, other hostelries, all of which provide snacks or more substantial meals, are the Ship Inn in West Street, the Rose and Crown adjacent to the Bookshop in the Market Place, the Angel Inn in St. Osyth's Lane just off the town centre, the Black Horse on Benefield Road and the George on Glapthorn Road. Other eating places can be found at several locations in and around the town.

From Drummingwell Lane turn right and at the crossroads opposite are the ***Palmer Chemistry block [10],*** with carved intertwined serpents on the wall, next to the Physics and Workshops blocks in Blackpot Lane. The lane was the site of a gasworks and a brewery in the 19th century. On the near corner of Milton and Glapthorn Roads is the ***Sir Peter Scott building [11],*** housing the Mathematics and Biology Departments and commemorating a renowned Old Oundelian.

At the junction turn left to see the ***Yarrow [12],*** given by Mr A.F. (later Sir Alfred) Yarrow in memory of his son Eric killed at Ypres in 1915. This gallery is now used as a venue for exhibitions by School staff and pupils and other local artists. More distant still are the boarding houses of **Sanderson** and ***Dryden [13],*** completed in the 1930s, the latter now a girls' house.

Opposite is the public library and emergency services and behind them, the old workhouse chapel, now converted to a private house but still retaining a magnificent painted ceiling. The next turning on the left is the gated private ***Pavilion Drive [14].*** Here are located the most recent of Oundle boarding houses, **Wyatt** and **Kirkeby**, separated by the new Sanatorium, together with the main cricket pitches and sports field. Note also the ***"Old San" [15],*** on the corner.

Alternatively turn left from Drummingwell Lane along Milton Road to see ***St. Anthony House, [16],*** *1920's,* with a four-sided copper dome. Opposite is the ***Chapel [17],*** built as memorial to Oundle School's 221 Old Boys fallen in the First World War. Inside is a remarkable organ by the Danish builder Frobenius, together with stained glass windows by John Piper who also designed the hangings behind the altar. Each summer an internationally renowned Organ Festival is held at the

School; also of musical "note" is the annual Oundle Music Festival held in the town during early May.

Next are more boarding houses, ***Sidney*** *and* ***Grafton [18],*** then ***Laxton*** *and* ***Crosby [19],*** all built in the early 20th century, next to the School Sports Hall and the ***Swimming Pool [20],*** which is open at times to Oundle residents. At the junction of Milton Road and Benefield Road are ***workshops [21],*** shown on the 1885 Ordnance Survey map as the site of an Infant's School. High up on the wall is an inscription on a diamond shaped plaque:

> ihs
> St Ann's
> in the
> GROVE
> 1862

Close by is the former Drill Hall, now used in part as ***Oundle Museum [22].*** Returning towards the town centre, on an island at the junction of four roads is the Roman ***Catholic Jesus Church [23].*** Near the corner of ***Stoke Hill is New House [24],*** a boarding house rebuilt in 1640 and near the now disused ***Old Courthouse [25].***

South down Mill Road are single storey ***workmen's*** **cottages [26],** dating from the 1600's and near the next corner in South Road is the old ***Anchor Brewery [27].*** Go over South Bridge to Barnwell Country Park and facing it across the road, Oundle Marina. On a little way is the attractive old Barnwell Mill, now a restaurant and adjacent to the Upper Barnwell guillotine lock. On the opposite side, is a gravel track with unofficial parking.

The Nene Way follows this to the Lower Barnwell lock, and from there back to Oundle across the water meadows.

Either return to the town centre via South Road to see views towards the Nene to the south or walk along West Street which is a shorter route. From South Road a footpath runs from ***Bassett Ford Road [28],*** across fields and footbridges to the Nene Way. Note the old ***Anchor Inn Cottage [29],*** on the corner of East Road with its low windows and partially sunken doorway. Continue along St. Osyth's Lane to return to the Market Place.

The optional and shorter route back to the Market Place takes you along West Street (originally High Street) which boasts antiques and other specialist shops. Set back from the road at Victoria Yard is the 1852 ***Baptist Chapel [30],*** now converted into flats. Opposite is Setchells Yard and the ***Manor House [31].***

Further along on the left in an old Congregational chapel, is Oundle School's ***Rodolphe Stahl Theatre [32],*** with a reputation for excellence. Across the other side of the road is ***Danfords [33],*** with its elaborate gateway.

A little further on the northern side are Paine's Cottage and The Manse, separated by a high walled garden with an ***ornamental gateway [34].*** The cottage was the town house of the Mildmay's of Apethorpe, and connected with Paine's Almshouses founded in 1801 by John Paine who gave four tenements to house families of protestant dissenters. At the far end of the original gardens, now in the grounds of the St. Anthony's boarding house and visible from Milton Road is an 18th

Entrance to Paine's Cottage

century gazebo with arched windows and a pyramid roof.

The Headmaster's house, ***Cobthorne [35],*** 1656, was built by Major-General William Butler, an aide to Oliver Cromwell. It has extensive gardens stretching down to South Road, (See also Lyveden). Opposite is the ***Victoria Hall [36],*** built at the turn of the 20th century, which houses council chambers and a civic hall. At the junction with New Street is ***Oundle's War Memorial [37],*** and across the road the Travel Information Centre.

To see more of the town, from the Market place take a diversion down St. Osyth's Lane and along East Road to see ***houses [38],*** with bricked-up windows on their frontage - probably a result of the infamous Window Tax of 1697 originally intended to contribute to funding the War of Spanish Succession. All house occupiers had to pay a levy of 2/- and an extra 8/- if there were between ten and twenty windows. The charge was repealed in 1851 when it was recognised that the health of the nation might matter as much as its wealth!

On the next corner a distant view of the original frontage of ***The Berrystead [39],*** now a preparatory boarding house for 11 to 13 year old girls and boys, with the spire of St. Peter's church beyond. Continue along East Road and turn left at the end past ***old maltings [40],*** returning to the town centre along the narrow North Street.

Houses in North Street display an amazing variety of architectural styles from 16th century onwards (don't miss the roofs and the doorways) including the still used ***Latham's Hospital "almshouses" [41],*** built in 1611, with an identical southern continuation in 1837. It was provided by benefactor Nicholas Latham (see Barnwell) and has over its gates the old Christian devices of a cross and a pelican on a nest. The most northerly entrance was until this century that to a Blue Coat school finally incorporated into other local schools as education reforms were enacted.

Next is ***Laundimer House [42],*** 19th century, then the Berrystead once more. The ***White Lion 1641 [43],*** *was* originally an Inn and until recently Laxton School's Headmaster's house. Along further is ***Laxton Junior School [44],*** rambling its way between here and East Road. On the opposite side of the road is an ***old mileage indicator [45],*** carved into the wall of the old rectory dating from the mid-19th century.

Mileage Indicator

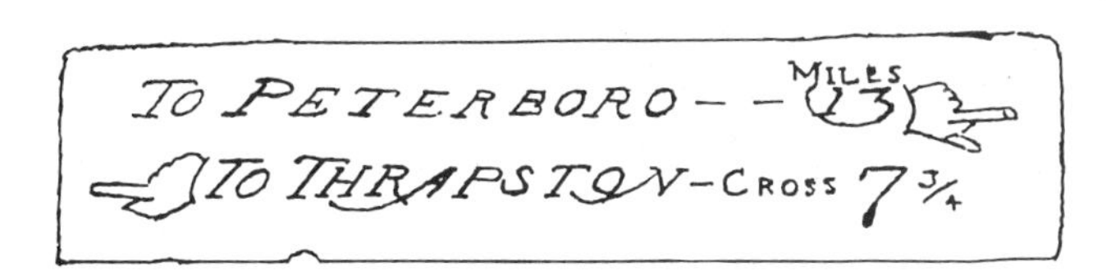

Nearby a marker ***"O/R's" [46],*** means what? The only thing the writer can surmise is "Other Ranks". With St. Peter's on your right, just before re-entering the Market Place notice the ***Jericho cul-de-sac [47],*** on the left, the name of which has not changed in 400 years.

The Churchyard [48], provides a fairly peaceful haven; its trees include walnut, beech and copper beech, horse chestnut and the inevitable yews. Grey squirrels are often to be seen and there is a large rookery, (one of several in the town), in the trees beyond the north wall. On the wall are a series of ***carved numbers [49].*** Various suggestions have been made as to their purpose; the most likely is that they mark rows of graves.

There is some evidence of an important Saxon church in the town and the present structure of St. Peter's Parish Church may have been built on the site from around the 13th century. Below the west window in the tower a carved Saxon stone may be seen and during recent work it was discovered that the interior pillars stand on earlier footings. The tower was constructed in the 14th and 15th centuries and the date 1634 is visible above the southern parapet, showing the date of the rebuilding of the spire.

Recently re-ordered internally, the grey Victorian stonework which had been stripped of its original plaster, has been reworked to provide a light, spacious, colourful and adaptable building. A magnificent polished wooden floor has been installed and the pews replaced by upholstered chairs which can be rearranged as required. At the same time features hidden for many years such as a Victorian reredos and medieval screens have been brought back into use to enhance active worship.

The lectern is Flemish; it and the porch are from the mid 15th century. The vestry and garderobe together with the fireplace were added later and indicate that it was intended as a priest's dwelling. Its modern-day replacement the Vicarage is a large three-storey building on New Street.

Beyond the immediate town centre north-eastwards along Station Road towards the A605 roundabout and the Peterborough road, the road crosses **North Bridge [50],** rebuilt after destruction by floods in 1570 and renovated since. Actually there are two bridges with separate inscriptions. That nearest the town:

IN
THE YERE OF
OVRE LORD 1570
THES ARCHES WER
BORNE DOVNE BY THE
WATERS EXTREMYTIE
IN THE YERE OF OVRE
LORD 1571 THEY WER
BVLDED AGAYN WITH
LYME AND STONNE
THANKS BE TO GOD

The London and North Western Railway (later the L.M.S. and then B.R.) ran through the Nene Valley and the second plaque is nearer the attractively converted old railway station built in 1845 and once described by Sir John Betjemen as "One of the finest examples of domestic railway station architecture in England". Rather less appealing than the former it relates to the rebuilding and widening of the structures between 1912 and 1914. The need for such a wide expanse of bridges is only apparent when the fields flood after heavy rain, sometimes threatening to encroach upon The Maltings elderly people's dwellings on the outskirts of the town.

A mile from the town centre north along the Glapthorn Road and at its junction with Rockingham Hills observe a stone with the words:

> THIS SPRING
> IS THE PROPERTY OF THE
> OUNDLE BOARD OF GUARDIANS
> WHO HAVE THE RIGHT OF
> ENTRY FOR REPAIRING IT
> AND THE PIPES WHICH PIPES
> LIE IN DIRECT LINE FROM
> THIS
> TO THE TANK NEAR THE ROAD
> 1849

Springs have always been an important water source in this district and many are still marked on the 1:25,000 Ordnance Survey Pathfinder Maps.

West of the town, along the A427 Benefield Road, is Oundle Golf Course and near the road, Biggin Fish Pond with Oundle Wood beyond. A right of way follows the southern boundary of this woodland. The road branches just beyond and the left fork, Harley Way, leads to Lyveden New Bield and Brigstock and to the right Weldon and Corby.

Footpaths to: Ashton, Barnwell Country Park, Cotterstock, Tansor, Nene Way

BARNWELL COUNTRY PARK

TL036873

Barnwell Country Park (TL036873) is set in 37 acres (15 ha) between Oundle and the A605. It contains walks through wood and meadow and has marsh and open water and is bounded to the west by the Nene. Over thirty bird species including the kingfisher breed here. There is a warden, information, occasional lectures, facilities for disabled fishermen; a picnic area and toilets. Don't miss the giant carved models of the stages of a dragonfly's life from chrysalis to on the wing, visible on the west side of the park. In wet weather you are advised to wear good footwear.

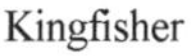

Kingfisher

Opposite the entrance to the Park is the Oundle Marina, mooring place for many river craft using the navigable River Nene.

St. John The Baptist, Achurch

SOUTH WEST

Achurch; Aldwincle; The Benefields; Brigstock; Lilford; Lowick; Lyveden New Bield; Pilton; Stoke Doyle; Sudborough; Thorpe Waterville; Wadenhoe.

ACHURCH TL022832 Population 128

Also known as Thorpe Achurch the village mainly consists of a row of identical estate cottages built from 1830-1840 running parallel with the A605. Of Saxon origin, there was an Iron Age and later Roman settlement here and a Roman Road passed nearby. Of special note is an oak canopy to the well in the village. It bears the inscription:

Commemorative Well-Head

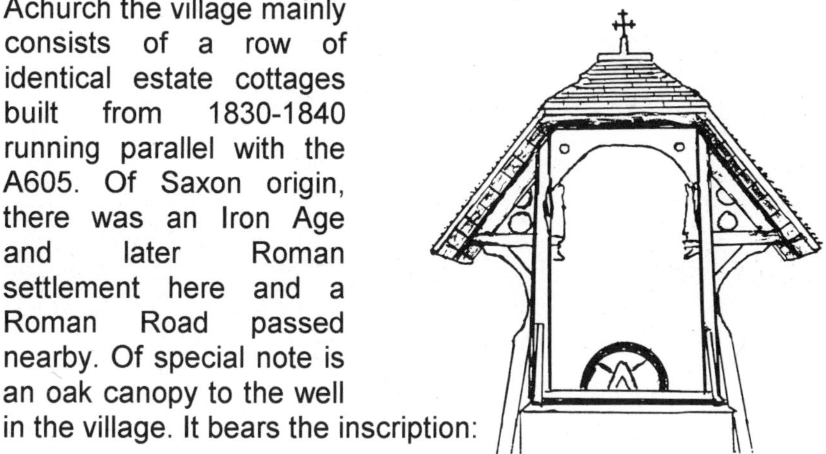

IN MEMORY OF THOMAS ALBERTON POWYS MDCCCLXXXII

Down the "no through road" is the church of St. John the Baptist with a 19th century interior. It is also the Parish Church for Wigsthorpe, Thorpe Waterville and Lilford. Surplus stone from the lost parish church of St.

Peter's in the latter village, was used by Sir Thomas, the first Lord Lilford, to effect repairs here.

Originally built in around 1300 and was constructed in the form of a cross as thanksgiving by Sir Asceline de Waterville for safe return from the Crusades. He lies buried near the main door. There is a large white marble monument inside.

The Nene Way passes through the churchyard and then skirts a walled orchard, before crossing the Nene by way of footbridges. At its entrance is a carved oak lychgate with an inscription on the front:

TO THE HONOUR AND GLORY OF GOD AND TO THE BELOVED MEMORY OF MY HUSBAND THOMAS LYTTLETON 4TH BARON LILFORD

At the bottom of Lynches Wood are the remains of St. Peter's, Lilford, which was demolished in 1778. Stone from it was used by Sir Thomas to build three arches (only one now intact) in this privately owned wood north of the existing church. Managed by the Forestry Commission, shooting parties take place. Take care, keep to the signposted right of way from the village towards Lilford Park (not open to the public) and observe the Country Code.

Footpaths to: Lilford, Wadenhoe, Nene Way

ALDWINCLE TL006818 Population 310

Variously spelt in a variety of guide books the name is in the Domesday Book as Eldewincle meaning a nook or corner. The village is sited at a double bend of the River Nene. A Roman bridge from the first century AD was discovered nearby on the boundary with Titchmarsh. A neolithic mortuary was excavated in 1968 and found to contain boat-shaped coffins and an Iron Age hut 37ft. in diameter and a ditch complex have also been found.

The village is almost unique in having two churches; particularly as the rectory of each was the birthplace of important literary figures. The 13th century church of All Saints contains a memorial to John Dryden (1631-1700) poet laureate under Charles II in spite of earlier associations with Cromwell. The Chambre Chapel was founded by the will of Elizabeth Chambre in 1489.

The church has been declared redundant but is kept in order; in its rectory Dryden was born. That building still stands renamed as Dryden House and a national flag may often be seen flying from the flagpole in the garden.

St. Peter's Church has a good example of a broach spire and attractive weathercock with a more delicate bird than is usual. Thomas Fuller was born at this rectory in 1608 although the building was destroyed in 1790, living on in name only as Rectory Field. There is also a Baptist Church in the main street, opened in 1823. In narrow Lowick Lane is Tavern Cottage and on its wall is a plaque dated 1834 with three castelated towers and apparently Masonic symbols. It was removed here in 1954 from the adjacent parish of Titchmarsh.

A Saxon track passes nearby and was in use until the middle ages as a coach route. The area has been known since the 15th century as a "conygher" or rabbit warren. A local spinney in a disused pit contains a large variety of deciduous and conifer trees and has been set aside as a Pocket Park. There are many public footpaths running from the village and evidence of strip cultivation in the fields off the Wadenhoe Road can be seen. There is a variety of housing ranging from 16th century thatched cottages to 20th century executive dwellings.

The village has connections with Titchmarsh and is the nearest village to the Titchmarsh Nature Reserve. Bounded by the River Nene and Harper's Brook this consists of 150 acres (73 hectares) of lakes and islands created from old gravel workings in the 1920's. There are bird-watcher's hides and the reserve is renowned for visits of migrating waders and geese and breeding pairs of plovers and oystercatchers. Kingfishers are quite common and wintering wildfowl are to be seen in large numbers.

On the site of a duck decoy created by Lord Lilford in 1885 there is an important heronry which is a Site of Special Scientific Interest. Visitors are asked not to enter the heronry as the birds can be easily disturbed. Also to be found are many wild flowers and species of insects including butterflies and dragonflies. There is a car park at the Aldwincle side of the reserve.

Footpaths to: Islip, Sudborough, Titchmarsh, Wadenhoe, Nene Way

BENEFIELD (UPPER and LOWER) **SP 988886**
Population 342

The Church of St. Mary is dated 1847 and given by the Watts-Russell family. The north screen is earlier from the 1700's and has a carved centre with the family coat of arms. The church is in Lower Benefield on the Brigstock road just off the main A427 which snakes its way through the village. Approached along a tree and cottage lined footpath through a lychgate, inside there is an ornate private gateway to Benefield House. It is the only churchyard the writer has come across with an electrified fence enclosing most of the graves! To the west of the church is a moated mound, the site of a former castle licensed in 1208 and derelict by 1315. Biggin Hall part way between Oundle and Upper Benefield dates from the 18th century with 20th century additions.

Between Lower and Upper Benefield and near to a public footpath which crosses the valley are swallow holes, typical features of limestone country, where a stream disappears underground. Equally common and found here too are springs where watercourses reappear. Another path intersects and leads west to Spring Wood and Fermyn Woods Hall. (See Brigstock). Yet another goes south through Banhaw Wood to Lyveden and a gated road leads from Lower Benefield to Glapthorn.

On the A427 from Corby to Oundle just west of Upper Benefield is an aircrew memorial to the USAAF's 401St Bombardment Group (Heavy) based at Deenethorpe Airfield from 1943 to 1945, which had a reputation for bombing accuracy. Just under 2900 men were based here and the group flew 7430 sorties, 254 missions and lost 94 of its B-17's with ten men on each aircraft, most of whom would have been teenagers or in their early twenties. This was the second lowest loss ratio in the 8th Air Force.

The former control tower still stands although in a dangerous condition. Panels from the air base chapel are now incorporated into the Church of St. Mary the Virgin, Weldon, near Corby. In the sixties the 6000ft. runway was resurfaced for British Steel's corporate jets and used till 1979. Walkers on the many rights of way should be aware that the airfield is still used occasionally for light aircraft. (See also Deenethorpe).

The Wheatsheaf in Upper Benefield, opposite the junction with the Glapthorn Road has a restaurant at the rear. In the pub is a silk escape map, photographs and other memorabilia to do with the nearby airfield.

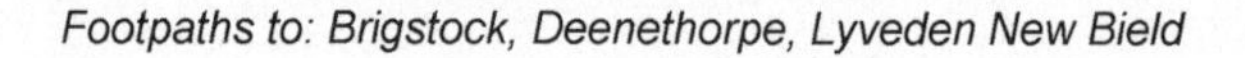

Footpaths to: Brigstock, Deenethorpe, Lyveden New Bield

Wartime control tower of a similar pattern to Deenethorpe.

BRIGSTOCK SP945853 Population 1260

A large community in the Middle Ages it was originally one of three bailiwicks of Rockingham Forest, an immense wooded area which covered a large section of the county. Deforestation came about because Charles I needed vast amounts of timber for his Navy. In spite of this logging is still an important part of the local economy and there is a sawmill in the centre of the village. Nearby is the old four-storey Wallis and Linnell's Mill, originally a clothing factory from 1873 and now an architectural practice. Local inns are the Green Dragon (with an oriental restaurant) and the Old Three Cocks, a coaching inn.

The church of St. Andrew started around 750 has a rare semi-circular stair turret which seems too large merely for a staircase. The nave is Saxon and the north aisle Norman. It was rebuilt in 1133 after destruction by the Danish invaders and a Lady chapel was added in mid 13th century, with the spire the next century. It was again ravaged, this time by Cromwell's men, during the Civil War. Inside is a monument to the first Lord Lyveden.

There is a sundial in the porch. At one time the church bell was tolled three times per day to guide travellers lost in the forest. As with other churches in the district there are beautifully embroidered kneelers in the pews.

The Manor is dated around 1150 reportedly used by King John in the early 13th century. There are Jacobean extensions and a staircase. The fireplace is mid 18th century.

Fermyn Woods Hall to the northeast was originally a 14th century hunting lodge, but had several later additions. In the grounds is a tall hexagonal well-head. Nearby is a County Council run Country Park on the site of a former sand pit with car parking, picnic areas, a warden and information service and a circular walk through what remains of Fermyn (Old English for "farming") Woods; the original timber having been sold by Charles I.

Running north from the Stanion Road along Old Dry Lane is a right of way which skirts the eastern edge of part of the old forest and the western side the Deer Park of Fermyn Woods Hall. This leads to Bocase Farm and a little further on the partially concealed 3ft (1m). Bocase Stone. This has two inscriptions relating to a former Bocase Tree thought by many to have been a site connected with archery and possibly visited by Robin Hood. Continuing along the path will go past Harry's Park Wood and link up with other public paths to the Benefield and Oundle Roads, or to a more westerly walk back through the woodland to Brigstock once again.

Brigstock Cross

Fotheringhay House in the village is partly built of stone from the demolished castle in the village of that name. Harper's Brook which flows past the spired church flows into the Nene at Aldwincle. In the thriving Middle Ages there was a weekly market; gone by 1623

it is now only recalled by the cross dated 1586. The disused watermill known as the Matchbox was built in 1873 of Weldon stone and has cast-iron window frames.

The War Memorial on Hall Hill, a conservation area, is on the site of an original Latham's Charity School. A track named Dusthill Road and Clay Dick leads by way of Geddington Chase to the village of that name just north of Boughton Park and Kettering.

Footpaths to: Deenethorpe, Lyveden, Geddington, Stanion, Wadenhoe

LILFORD-CUM-WIGSTHORPE TL033837 Population 68

Of Saxon origin, the village was depopulated by Sir Thomas Powys in 1775 in order that he might create Lilford Park of 240 acres, unfortunately no longer open to the public. The people were rehoused in the Viking settlement of Wigsthorpe. (Wykingthorpe in 13th century).

Lilford Hall was built around 1635 and was a Jacobean Place of Merit. The south front is of that date and the interior by Sir Thomas Powys from 1711 together with an ornate row of thirteen chimneys connected by arches. The entrance hall is around 1730 and the designs for it are held in the County Record Office. The ballroom is Victorian.

Lilford Bridge

Note also the fine "mirror image" gatehouse on the road from Pilton to the Thrapston to Peterborough Road. This road crosses over the fine stone Lilford Bridge, best seen from the river.

Footpaths to: Achurch, Pilton, Nene Way

LOWICK SP977810 Population 252

Sited on the east bank of Harper's Brook with attractive views across the valley, it is mainly comprised of stone cottages, (many thatched) and was part of the Drayton Estate to the south east. Drayton House dates back to 1328 but has been much altered over succeeding centuries. Above the State Bedroom is a priest's hole; this may be connected with the time when the occupier, the fourth Lord Mordaunt of Turvey was involved in the Gunpowder Plot. There is much else to discover here; of particular note is the ironwork gates and supports.

St. Peter's Church, Lowick

In Drayton Road, Lowick, is a former school founded in 1720 by Sir John and Lady Germaine for twenty poor children. The Snooty Fox public house has a reputation for good food.

The Perpendicular church of St. Peter was built in the 14th century at the expense of Sir Henry Greene, then owner of Drayton Hall. On the side of a hill it has a pinnacled tower with an octagonal lantern similar to that at Fotheringhay. The hall has a Tudor chimney, Elizabethan towers and Edwardian battlements and is built on the site of a former castle.

Footpaths to: Drayton Park, Islip, Slipton, Sudborough

Lyveden New Bield

LYVEDEN SP983852

Well worth a visit, the roofless country house known as Lyveden New Bield was built in the shape of a cross, with Christian emblems carved around its walls, by Sir William Tresham in 1594. Access is by footpath from the Harley Way, the Oundle to Brigstock Road. A small fee is levied by the National Trust who have the property in their care. Park off the single track road in the extended lay-by near Lyveden Manor.

The Treshams were implicated in the Gunpowder Plot (See Pilton) and Sir William had severe financial difficulties. He was to die in prison with his masterpiece unfinished. To the north is Lyveden Old Bield which was remodelled by Sir Thomas Tresham from 1604. It was to become the main Tresham property after confiscation of land in direct result of the notorious Plot. The gateway is now incorporated into Fermyn Woods Hall. (See Brigstock).

Nearby is a water garden, the site of a confrontation between disenchanted Scottish mutineers from the Black Watch and English Dragoons in the early eighteenth century. Five companies of the Scotsmen had been commanded to join George II's army and go to Flanders.

Around 140 of them believed they should only fight on their native soil and were attempting to make their way back north when surrounded at Lady Wood, part of the dense Rockingham Forest, north of Sudborough. They encamped in the nearby garden and sent a message to

Major John Creed, residing at Cobthorne, West Street, Oundle, that they were prepared to surrender. Most gave themselves up; all were eventually sentenced to death. In the event all but three were eventually deported to the colonies. The ringleaders were shot at the Tower of London.

Beware! A low-level training route for military aircraft means they can fly very low and often very fast over this site which is probably used as a navigational waymark.

Footpaths to: Lower Benefield, Wadenhoe

Tornado over Lyveden

PILTON TL024846 Population 63

There is a Manor House (not open to the public) formerly owned by the Tresham family which has in part been built over the graveyard of the Parish Church in this small hamlet northwest of Lilford Park. It was enlarged about 1620 with an imposing Jacobean staircase and a first- floor Great Chamber. At one time both the house and Lilford Hall belonged to Sir Thomas Powys and oak panelling from the Hall was removed to Pilton Manor. Outside the garden is formally laid out with yew hedges and croquet hoops at the front and a long high box hedge to the rear.

Some of the preliminary meetings of the Gunpowder Plot were held in the house. There is some evidence of a secret room, last seen in the 1890's but there is no suggestion it was linked to the Plot. In the 1840's the Manor House was given to the Church in exchange for the old rectory. It was then sold on in the mid 20th century to private owners.

The Bede House Watch Tower

Other houses in the village have medieval fragments as at the three-storey building by the meadow gates. This is the Bede House also known as the Old Watch House.

What at first appears to be redbrick chimney on closer inspection can be seen to contain a window. It may have been used as a watch-tower by the outlawed Catholic Treshams. A Victorian Postbox may be seen in the wall of one house.

The Church of St. Mary and All Saints is mainly 12th and 13th centuries with the chancel rebuilt in 1862. The spire and tower were restored in 1896 and all four bells date from the 16th century. There are late Victorian tiles probably bestowed by the fourth Lord Lilford who was responsible for the Lilford Aviaries at the end of the 19th century. The Church is reached by a footpath from village.

Footpaths to: Lilford, Stoke Doyle

St. Rumbold's Church, Stoke Doyle

STOKE DOYLE TL027863 Population 64

The greystone houses of this small village are reminiscent of Wales. The church of St. Rumbold is plain in aspect with clear-glass leaded windows and was built from 1722-25 on an isolated mound overlooking a virtually dry stream. Two carved angels either side of the east window are c.1835.

Public footpaths run past both sides of the church down Hatchdoyle Lane and Church Lane towards, but not reaching, the River Nene. Opposite the road to the church is the Shuckburgh Arms offering good food and bed and breakfast accommodation. To the west, behind the inn is Sevenwells Spring.

A Manor House is to the south east of the village adjacent to old fish ponds. Its 18th century gates have been removed to East Haddon Hall. A dry moat is near to the L-shaped old rectory, 1633, along Church Lane.

Footpaths to: Pilton and towards Harley Way and Brigstock

SUDBOROUGH SP968821 Population 138

A small village, built on the north bank of Harper's Brook it lies north of Lowick, at the centre of the old Rockingham Forest. On the old turnpike entrance to the village from the south is a circular former toll-house dated 1660, subsequently used as a public house but now a private dwelling. Today's local hostelry is the thatched Vane Arms in the main street.

The church is All Saints built mainly in the 13th century. It has a carved pulpit. Thatched cottages are in much evidence, with some surprises. There is a right of way running south to Islip and Thrapston along the course of the brook. The author "B.B." (Denis Watkins-Pitchford) lived here.

Mileage indicator on the gatepost of All Saints Church

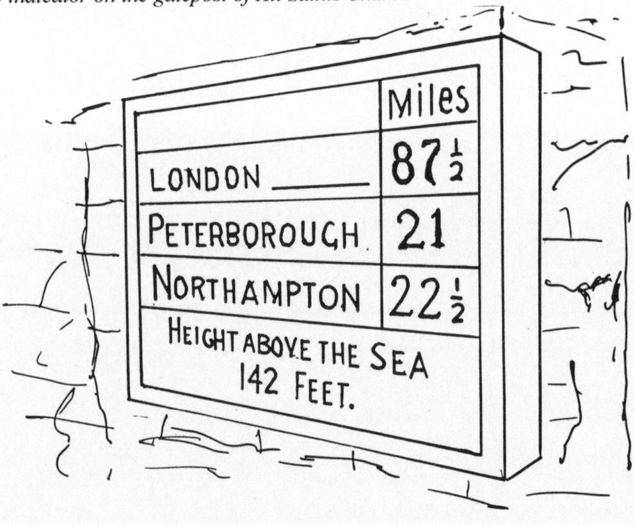

Northeast of the village is a large tract of woodland reached by track and public footpath and from there, Lyveden New Bield. Along the Brigstock road is another path which leads up across open country to Fermyn Woods and the Harley Way. To the south is Drayton Park.

Footpaths to: Islip, Lowick, Slipton, Wadenhoe

THORPE WATERVILLE TL024816

This was an early Danish settlement and the remains of a later castle which was probably no more than a fortified manor, together with an associated church destroyed in the Wars of the Roses survive but are now pressed into use as a barn.

The bridge across the brook is early 14th century with ribs under the arches. The Fox Inn on the main road offers food to weary travellers.

The Rev Robert Browne, founder of congregationalism, lived here and is commemorated by a plaque attached to the wall of his cottage. Traces of the old LNWR railway and station on the Peterborough to Northampton line are still visible.

Footpaths to: Titchmarsh

WADENHOE TL008833 Population 99

There has been a water mill here since Saxon times and the village name derives from Waden, a ford and Hoe, a hill. The old mill has been converted to private dwelling. The remaining pub is the King's Head with a back garden which stretches down to the river. Adjacent is a car park with access to the Nene Way and the public footpath to the Church and Aldwincle. Wadenhoe House, 1657 and rebuilt 1858 is now a conference centre. It boasts a circular limestone dovecote with 500 nest boxes.

Built in the mid 13th century and previously dedicated to St. Giles, the Parish Church of St. Michael and All Angels is perched on the side of a hill with the north entrance needing five steps down into the aisle. Castle Close on the north side shows evidence of a defensive rampart around the hilltop.

The church has a saddle-back tower possibly on Saxon foundations with a Collyweston tiles roof and a peal of six bells ranging from 1603 to 1937. There is a 13th century ornamented font set on an octagonal base. The church is still very much in use as a place of worship and as a witness to the glory of God.

Within the church is a memorial to Thomas and Caroline Welch-Hunt murdered by Italian bandits whilst honeymooning in 1824 and a stained glass window recalling the Rt. Hon. George Ward-Hunt, Chancellor of the Exchequer and First Lord of the Admiralty at the end of the 19th century.

Footpaths to: Achurch, Aldwincle, Islip, Sudborough, Thrapston, Titchmarsh, Nene Way

St. Michael and All Angels, Wadenhoe

NORTH AND WEST

Apethorpe; Blatherwycke; Bulwick; Cotterstock; Deene and Deenethorpe; Eaglethorpe; Elton; Fotheringhay; Glapthorn; Kings Cliffe; Laxton; Nassington; Southwick; Tansor; Woodnewton; Yarwell.

APETHORPE TL025957 Population 190

The Church is St. Leonard's, rebuilt in 1480 by the owner of the Hall but with 12th century work evident. The South Chapel is a memorial added in 1621 to Sir Anthony and Lady Grace Mildmay and their effigies lie there on a black and white marble tomb. The Chapel has a fine stained-glass window of 1621. Wall paintings are partly visible and the church clock is an example of an early pendulum version circa 1704 by John Watts. The East Window has recently been restored and is a rare example of painted rather than stained glass. Each wooden pew is adorned by delightful kneelers which have been embroidered by members of the parish.

In the churchyard is a War Graves Commission headstone to Flight Lieutenant E R Lewendon who, as Commanding Officer of 1426 Flight RAF, responsible for testing captured enemy aircraft, crashed near the village on October 13th 1944, whilst flying a Focke-Wulf 190. Opposite the church are old stocks and whipping post in an alcove of a wall.

Stocks and Whipping Post

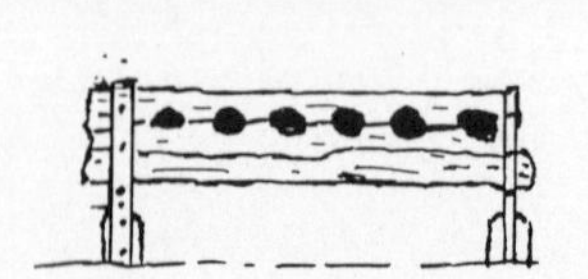

The Hall adjacent to the church belonged to Sir Guy Wolston in 1491 and by Sir Walter Mildmay in 16th century. It was bought by Leonard Brassey, M.P., later Lord Brassey, in 1904. Although not open to the public it provides a pleasant aspect and is best seen when entering the village from the south across the hump backed bridge over the Willow Brook, a tributary of the Nene. Built around two courtyards it has been successively added to from the 16th to the 18th centuries.

In the grounds of the Hall and thus not available to the general public lie the remains of a Roman Villa excavated in 1859. Collyweston slate was the roofing material and coins found indicate occupation around the 4th century AD.

In the mid 15th century many of the mostly thatched cottages were part of the manorial estate of Sir Guy Wolston. The Kings Head pub, on the Kings Cliffe road, next to an unattractive castellated tower thought to be a former dovecote, is worth a visit. Much of the village is now a conservation area.

Footpaths to: Kings Cliffe, Nassington, Yarwell, Brigstock

BLATHERWYCKE SP974958 Population 70

The village is in the ecclesiastical parish of Bulwick but Holy Trinity Church has been declared redundant. It has a Norman tower and south doorway. Inside are monuments to Sir Humphrey Stafford and his wife, who built Blatherwycke Hall in 1713 and probably Kirby Hall as well. The Staffords married into the O'Brien family and the Staffords love-knot may be seen on many buildings in the village. The Hall had to be pulled down in 1948 after irreparable damage caused by billeted troops in WWII. In a field nearby is a statue of the Apollo Belvedere which once graced the gardens; almost the only remnant of the once magnificent Hall.

Holy Trinity Church

The lake has several species of wildfowl but please note there is no access for bird watchers. It was dug by Irish labourers and is the largest man-made lake in the county. At its south end it is crossed by a bridge dated 1656. Stables to the north east are dated 1770.

The church is preserved by English Heritage although closed to the public. It is however off the beaten track, surrounded by woods and accessible by dirt roads or footpaths. The churchyard is unkempt, yet there is a solitary peace about the place and a seat to sit quietly and contemplate things spiritual.

Stafford's and O'Brien's Love-Knot on Blatherwycke Bridge

Footpaths to: Bulwick, Fineshade, Kings Cliffe, Wakerly

BULWICK SP963943 Population 151

Between Blatherwycke and Deene, set on the south side of the Willow Brook valley, the village is pleasant in aspect with much of its land owned by Bulwick Hall and almost all buildings pre-war. The Hall was constructed in 1676 and reworked in the mid 18th century. The Queens Head public house is dated 1683.

The Queen's Head

St. Nicholas' Church has a tall spire and a late 13th century chancel. Its first rector was appointed in 1227. There is a memorial to Admiral Tryon, a member of the family which owned the village, who perished at sea in 1893. The remaining male heirs were wiped out in the Great War. The ecclesiastical parish includes Blatherwycke.

Just over two miles north east of the village is Fineshade Abbey. Originally an Augustinian priory it was destroyed in 1749 and the Georgian mansion was demolished in 1956. There are 18th century stables and the earthworks of a pre 13th century castle are visible.

Footpaths to: Apethorpe, Blatherwycke, Deene, Harringworth

Cotterstock Mill and Bridge

COTTERSTOCK TL049905 Population 119

The village is mentioned in the Domesday Book and a Roman villa was excavated here in the 18th century. There have been two manors. One was granted a medieval chantry college of priests by Queen Isabella in 1338. The second, Cotterstock Hall, dating from around 1656 was frequented by the poet Dryden who wrote his "Fables" here whilst staying with his cousin. It was later altered and the staircase is from the 19th century.

A hump-backed bridge crosses the Nene on the approach to the village from the east and there is a fine house with a large cedar tree, on the double bend. It overlooks a weir and sluice of the Nene and the restored and non-functioning corn mill nearby. Lord Cardigan of Deene had a private wharf built here in 1729,

There are footpaths to Oundle to the south along both sides of the river and views of the Church from the bridge. There is a medieval cross at the junction of the road which leads to the church.

St. Andrews church is a mixture of styles with a decorated chancel looking towards the Nene. It was built by John Gifford, Canon of York in connection with the founding of a college in 1338. The interior stonework was stripped in a restoration of 1877. A Regency house opposite the rectory of 1720 has an ironwork verandah.

Footpaths to: Oundle, Tansor

DEENE AND DEENETHORPE SP952928 (Deene)
Population 86

These are two estate villages of Deene Park on opposite sides of the Willow Brook. The house has been the home of the Brudenell family, descendents of the Earl of Cardigan since the 16th century. Many properties are still occupied by estate workers.

The church of St. Peter (in Deene) dates from the 12th century and was restored in 1868 by Lady Adeline Cardigan in memory of her husband Lord James Cardigan who led the Charge of the Light Brigade.

Little is left of the original medieval parts of Deene Park House except for the great hall with its hammerbeam roof which was completed in around 1570. It has a collection of Crimean memorabilia on display and is open to the public on some summer Sundays. The lake was added to the estate by the third Earl.

Every one of the 32 limestone cottages in Deenthorpe, across the valley, were damaged when an American B-17 Flying Fortress bomber crashed into a cottage on take off from the airfield in December 1943 and its bomb load exploded. No one was seriously injured in the village although the blast was heard in Kettering twelve miles away.

Footpaths to: Apethorpe, Benefield, Brigstock, Bulwick, Glapthorn, Weldon

EAGLETHORPE TL076916

Although really a hamlet of Warmington, it lies to the west of our A605 divide. The name is probably Scandinavian in origin. On the Roman Road it thrived until the 16th century but was depopulated when Elton Park was enlarged.

Dovecote at Eaglethorpe

There are stone houses in the hamlet and a medieval dovecote with 797 nesting boxes (now a listed Ancient Monument) stands in the private grounds of Eaglethorpe Farm. In the middle ages the eggs and birds were important sources of protein. The dovecote can be seen well from the Nene Way footpath which runs past the mill.

There has been a mill here at least since the Domesday Book was compiled and Warmington Mill had its own wharf. The backwater is now the location for Elton Boat Club.

Eaglethorpe House is 17th century with a door and its surround probably removed from Fotheringhay Castle. The hawk in a fetterlock is the emblem of Edward IV.

Footpaths to: Elton, Fotheringhay, Nene Way

Warmington Mill, Eaglethorpe

ELTON TL089936 Population 623

The site of Elton Hall has been occupied since the Norman Conquest. Today it is some 200 acres and the Hall itself contains furniture and paintings from 15th century. Sir Thomas Proby arrived in 1665 and set about extensive restoration.

The library holds Henry VIII's prayer book and other rare works and a State Coach from Queen Victoria's jubilee is here. The Hall is open most Bank Holiday weekends and guided tours are available. It has recently had extensive refurbishment and decoration of many state rooms including the dining room and picture gallery.

There are two pubs, the Black Horse Inn on the main "through" road is over 200 years old and its basement was occasionally used to house prisoners until they could be taken on to Huntingdon. The Crown Inn dates from the early 17th century to which a recent and attractive round restaurant has been added at the rear. Additionally the Loch Fyne seafood restaurant is in the old dairy near the bypass.

The Church stands in a large, well kept and peaceful graveyard. It was begun in 1270 but, like Oundle, there are traces of Saxon foundations. Chancel, nave arcades and the north aisle were rebuilt early in the 14th century. The north vestry (sacristy) was added later. Much of the south arcade dates from around 1460 and forty years later the imposing west tower, now containing a peal of five bells, was begun. Medieval scratch dials can be seen at the entrance to the south porch which dates from 1505.

Under the direction of William Proby, the 5th Earl, restoration of the building occurred in the late 19th century and an organ chamber constructed. The Lady Chapel contains a statue of the Blessed Virgin Mary from the church of St. Nicholas, Birmingham, destroyed in the second world war.

The south-west window is by William Morris to a design by Dante Gabriel Rossetti, the English poet and painter. A window in the tower of the martyrdom of St. Stephen is by Sir Edward Burne-Jones, another British painter and friend of both Morris and Rossetti.

There are other fine windows, and mural tablets paying tribute to members of the Proby family. The oak pulpit and lectern were given by Rev F.W. Faber, a former rector who later converted to Roman Catholicism with John Henry Newman.

In 1912 the Elton Hall Fire Brigade was used to pump thousands of gallons of water into the foundations to prevent the drying out of the clay soil and subsidence of the foundations.

Opposite the church is Cooper's Hospital, an almshouse for four women of "poore, aged and needy circumstances of pious and goode character of the toune of Elton". On the wall of a building nearby is a unique French-style memorial to Joscelyn, Baroness Lewal, "who died .... on 13th June 1917 aged 29 years", a member of the Resistance. The inscription reads "She was ready".

Footpaths to: Fotheringhay, Nassington, Warmington, Yarwell

Roadside Shrine, Elton

FOTHERINGHAY TL060932 Population 113

This village is steeped in history and was the birthplace of Richard III in 1452 and the place of execution for Mary Stuart, Queen of Scots, on 8th February 1585. The Domesday Book speaks of Fodringea, an enclosure, which would have been an oasis in the sea of Rockingham Forest.

A castle was founded in the 12th century and rebuilt in the 14th. After the death of Mary the castle fell into disuse and was eventually demolished in 1628. The stone was reused in properties in the village and farther afield. Now only the castle mound remains close by the river and may be visited in daylight hours.

St. Mary and All Saints, Fotheringhay

The church of St. Mary and All Saints has strong connections with the House of York and is a landmark for miles around. Approached from the south along the road from Tansor obtains the best view of its flying buttresses and octagonal lantern tower graced with a golden-coloured weather vane of a falcon encircled by a fetterlock; the emblem of York, (See also Tansor).

The building founded in 14th century was truncated when its attached college and choir, was pulled down in 1548 by Dudley, Duke of Northumberland, for doubtful reasons. It was visited by Queen Elizabeth I in 1573. Buried within is Cicely Neville, mother of Edward IV. Rumour has it that music or singing may occasionally be heard coming from inside the empty church.

The remainder of the village is worth exploring. Particularly note the old forge, the well appointed Falcon Inn and Garden Farm with its Gothic arch. It is said that Bull, Mary's executioner stayed here. To the west Perio Mill near flooded gravel pits and the former village of Perio has a trout fishery, a gun supplier and a country clothing outlet.

Footpaths to: Elton, Nassington, Nene Way, Warmington, Woodnewton

GLAPTHORN TL024902 Population 277

Variously spelt on road signs and maps of the district with and without a trailing "e", names in the district seem to be based on Saxon field names influenced by later Roman occupation. The manor has been occupied by the Brudenell family since the 16th century; parish fields were enclosed in 1815.

The church of St. Leonard's is mostly 13th century and has a squat tower. The columns of the entrance porch lean severely and all but one window is clear leaded glass. Inside are several wall paintings and a Jacobean pulpit.

South Porch, St. Leonard's, Glapthorn

KINGS CLIFFE TL007971 Population 972

As its name implies the village was a Royal Manor, one of three bailiwicks of Rockingham Forest. Like its counterpart, Brigstock, its medieval market fell into disuse with the passage of time. The village was all but razed to the ground by Roundheads in the civil war. The Cross Keys public house has that sign carved on the outside. It is dated 1732 but thought to be older.

The dominant building material is Collyweston stone. The church is All Saints and St. James' set in attractive rural setting in the middle of the village. It has a Norman tower and 13th century spire. Some fragments of stained glass from Fotheringhay are visible.

The church room was once part of the water mill and the Willow Brook still flows beneath. Contained within are village archives and photographs of a bygone age. The book collection of William Law, clergyman and benefactor, is in Library House on School Hill.

The Manor House frontage is early 17th century with older parts elsewhere and a 19th century staircase. It is situated on Main Street.

There was a USAAF base here during the second World War with 1,400 personnel and almost 15,000 sorties (flights) were recorded. Initially the 56th Fighter Group (FG) trained on P-47 Thunderbolts. Later the 20th FG flew 312 combat missions on daylight bomber escort duty to the continent in P-38 Lightnings and then P-51 Mustangs. As at Deenethorpe the control tower still stands but is derelict and in a dangerous condition.

During the latter part of the war German P-O-W's were employed around the field. An unusual memorial to the base personnel, with a stone replica of the wings of a P-51, a Spitfire and the twin-boom P-38, surrounded by unit badges may be seen on the Wansford Road.

Footpaths to: Apethorpe, Blatherwycke, Bulwick, Fineshade, Fotheringhay, Nassington, Southwick, Yarwell

Kingscliffe Airfield Monument

LAXTON TL950960 Population 154

The village was rebuilt by the Lord Carbery, a member of the Evans family, starting around the turn of the 19th century; he also restored the exterior of the church of All Saints. Much of the building is 13th century but the north arcade in from the 19th. The pulpit was carved by Lord Carbery.

Laxton Hall was built in the early 19th century. A former orangery has been converted into a chapel. In the grounds is Laxton Park House of a gothic design.

Footpaths to: Fineshade, Gretton, Kings Cliffe, Wakerley

NASSINGTON TL063963 Population 672

In the 13th century prebends (revenues) of Lincoln Cathedral founded the Prebendal Manor House, thought to be the earliest surviving residence in Northamptonshire. Now in the care of English Heritage it has a 16th century Dovecote and Tithe Barn. Excavations in the grounds have found what are thought to be the foundations of a Royal Manor of King Canute dating from 10th century. The Manor House to the north is c.1500.

Prebendal Manor House

Gravel extraction in 1942 unearthed an Anglo-Saxon cemetery in pits near the river. Artefacts from here are now in Peterborough Museum. The church is St. Mary's and All Saints with a Saxon nave and late Norman tower. The aisles are 13th century and the broached spire is dated 1640. Inside the church is an Anglo-Saxon cross-shaft fragment and mid-14th century wall paintings.

Nassington's two pubs are the Queens Head which offers accommodation and has moorings for river craft and the Black Horse with a popular restaurant attached.

Lectern in St. Mary and All Saints, Nassington

Footpaths to: Elton, Fotheringhay, Kings Cliffe, Nene Way

SOUTHWICK TL021921 Population 161

Southwick Hall dates from the 14th century and was built by Sir John Knyvett, Lord Chancellor to Edward III, who also had a town house in Oundle. Subsequently the Lynn family took up residence. It has two stair turrets and rooms from the original house, a south wing added in the reign of Queen Elizabeth I and further parts constructed in 18th and 19th century.

On summer weekends eleven rooms of the Hall and the grounds are open to the public. Two of these are given over to an exhibition of Victorian clothes, together with children's toys and other items of interest. In the stable block are displays of carpentry and farming implements plus reconstructions of a cottage kitchen and a maids bedroom.

The church of St. Mary's is adjacent to the Hall and was built by the Knyvett family in about 1230 with the spire added by Sir John in 1350. It was rebuilt in the 18th century. The Shuckburgh Arms is the village's public house and is believed to date from the 1500's.

Southwick Wood to the north was once a spur of Rockingham Forest. To the south is Shortwood Nature Reserve of 62 acres, renowned for its display of bluebells in early May and conserved by the Northamptonshire Wildlife Trust. Over thirty bird species breed here regularly. Access is from the bridleway from the Glapthorn Road near the water tower at the top of Southwick Hill.

Footpaths to: Apethorpe, Perio Mill, Woodnewton

TANSOR TL053908 Population 161

This is a secretive village of high greystone walls and dense trees with few visible attractions. There was a pre-Roman settlement here and it was mentioned in the Domesday Book as Tanesovre.

The Church of St. Mary dates from at least the 11th century but with Norman piers of two kinds. Later amendments were made in the 13th and 14th centuries. Inside are misericords with emblems of the House of York; a falcon and a fetterlock. (See also Fotheringhay). The churchyard is lapped by the flooded Nene on occasions.

At the rear of the old Post Office, now a private dwelling, stands one of the village's two bakehouses complete with ovens. Also visible on private property and near to grazing land is an old sail-less windmill. Tansor Manor and Manor Farm on the Fotheringhay road are privately owned.

Footpaths to: Cotterstock, Oundle, Nene Way, Warmington

WOODNEWTON TL032946 Population 411

Woodnewton is mentioned in the Domesday Book as Newstone with a Manor House from 1730. St. Mary's Church has a 16th century tower with pillars from the late 12th and early 14th. The porch was remodelled in 1662 and the north aisle was destroyed in the same century. The whole structure was restored in the 19th and early 20th centuries.

With the emphasis on conservation the churchyard has been recognised as a wildlife haven of limestone grassland with its characteristic plants like birdsfoot trefoil and hoary plantain. To that end certain parts of it are managed to provide a sanctuary for bats, birds and flowers, (See also Nassington).

An old Wesleyan chapel has been converted into artists' workshops and studios. The White Swan Inn is located in Main Street and serves an a la carte and bar menu. There are ancient ash trees nearby.

Coco the Clown retired to the village and is buried in the churchyard. His headstone has a small bust of this famous Russian with an ambition to make people laugh. Part of the inscription reads:

IN LOVING MEMORY OF
NICOLAI POLAKOVS O.B.E.
(COCO THE CLOWN)

Coco was a founder member with Stan Bult of Clowns International and he only worked as a regular member of Roberts Brothers circus after he "retired" in 1969. Every two years since 1990, Woodnewton has held a "Clownfest" originally to raise money to build and equip a new Village Hall. Around 5000 people attend this one-day event in September and can meet internationally renowned clowns and get involved with the fun themselves.

Footpaths to: Elton, Fotheringhay, Southwick

YARWELL TL071978 Population 248

There is an ancient iron-ore quarry possibly of Roman origin, nearby in old Sulehay Forest. Across the Nene Valley is Sibson Airfield, originally a satellite of Peterborough and was used by the RAF from 1940-46 for night flying training with Airspeed Oxfords. 603 RAF and 37 WAAF personnel were based there. Today flying training and parachuting courses are run and aircraft are often seen climbing out to the west over the village.

Much of Northamptonshire is on limestone and there are old workings nearby. The 13th century church of St. Mary Magdalene has a tower remodelled in the 18th. The aisles were demolished in 1782. The interior contains a black marble tombstone commemorating Sir Humphrey Bellamy.

There is a camping and caravanning site by the river and the Angel Inn offers a place for relaxation. In a quarry in Yarwell parish but west of Wansford on the Kings Cliffe Road is the site of a Roman building, possibly a bailiff's house.

Footpaths to: Apethorpe, Nassington, Sibson, Wansford, Nene Way

EAST

Ashton; Barnwell; Caldecote; Clopton; Great Gidding; Hemington; Luddington; Lutton; Morborne; Polebrook; Thurning; Warmington; Winwick.

ASHTON TL055884 Population 104

The village is picturesque and is clustered around the village green and the well-frequented Chequered Skipper pub, named after a now-extinct local butterfly. Around the walls are collections of lepidoptera and other insects. In October each year the increasingly popular World Conker Championship is held here.

Lord Charles Rothschild founded the society that was to develop into today's Royal Society for Nature Conservation. His daughter Miriam, a foremost expert on insect life, has continued the family tradition for conservation in the woods of Ashton Wold. The house was built in 1900 in Tudor style for the family. The associated farms now in part produce wild-flower and grass seed as a viable crop. Some of the oaks are around 200 years old and many different species of flora and fauna are to be found.

The Wold is a private estate though rights of way do pass through it. The Nene Way footpath runs from Ashton to Fotheringhay. It passes adjacent to a rifle range and care should be exercised. There is a pleasant walk past Ashton Mill across the Nene floodplain to the historic town of Oundle. The mill is on the Oundle to Polebrook road and is on a Domesday site. It was converted by Lord Rothschild to provide water and electricity to Ashton village via underground cables and piping. It now contains a fish and bygones museum and is currently awaiting restoration.

Some settlement was here previous to the Rothschild era and Ashton chapel and school on the Nene Way is dated 1706. During WWII the woods were used by the military and even today many concrete structures still remain. Rather older relics of prehistoric, Iron Age and Roman periods have been found.

Although originally older, the 32 thatched cottages were rebuilt in the same Tudor style by Lord Rothschild around 1903. Each of them had the rarity of a bathroom installed at the time.

Footpaths to: Oundle, Nene Way, Warmington

BARNWELL TL049850 Population 390

What is now one village was described as a town in the Middle Ages with a weekly market, annual fair and an assize. It was made up of two parishes of St. Andrew's and of All Saints and contained seven wells, reputedly with healing properties for young children.

The largest structure in the village is Barnwell Manor, set in delightful gardens and home of the Duke and Duchess of Gloucester until 1995. The castle was built by Berengar Le Moyne around 1266 and the Manor sometime later. The estate was then sold to Ramsey Abbey. In 1540 Henry VIII granted it to Sir Edward Montagu who became Baron Montagu of Boughton in 1621.

When the male family line died out it passed through the female line to the Duke of Buccleuch until 1913 and then through various owners until the late Duke of Gloucester bought it in 1938. He changed the name from Castle to Manor although the site actually contains both castle and manor house. The castle, with its square plan and round corner towers has an eastern gatehouse with two round towers. It has occasionally been open to the public. The adjacent Medieval Barn has a Jacobean stone facade.

The village is bisected by Barnwell Brook which is crossed by eleven bridges and a ford. Virtually tame wildfowl can be found on the banks and the stream flows from the south through a flood storage reservoir built in 1990 after flooding caused much damage in recent decades. The older cottages in this attractive village are built of local stone often thatched or roofed with Collyweston slate. The Montagu Arms, by the hump-backed main road bridge has a pleasant garden area and is worth a visit.

Entrance Archway to Parson Latham's Cottages, Barnwell

Latham's Cottages, almshouses opposite St Andrew's Church, were generously given by the vicar, Rev Nicholas Latham, son of the keeper of Brigstock Great Park, in 1604, for fourteen poor people. Latham was Vicar here for 51 years. (See the long and informative plaque on the wall and also Oundle and Brigstock). The houses were rebuilt in 1874 and are still in use. Above the arched entrance is an inscription:

CAST THY BREAD UPON THE WATERS

The Parish Church is St. Andrew's. Externally it is mostly 13th century with the chancel remodelled in 1851. There is a memorial to Rev Nicholas Latham and also to Prince William of Gloucester, tragically killed when his Piper Twin Comanche, G-AWOG crashed during an air race in 1973. To the left of the main doorway are the remains of an old wall, now giving access to the Rectory. Behind the church is a conservation area for plants and wildlife.

On the western side of the brook the chancel of All Saints still stands, occasionally used and containing memorials to the Montagu family, the Earls of Sandwich. The remainder was demolished in 1825 due to structural weakness.

Along the Polebrook Road are Barnwell Workshops affording a location for light industry. On the Oundle Road is Barnwell Mill built in 1746 and now a popular restaurant adjacent to one of the Nene locks. The Railway followed the line of the present Oundle bypass and the Station was built in 1845 in Old-English style. It is now a private house.

Footpaths to: Armston, Luddington, Polebrook, Thurning, Titchmarsh, Wigsthorpe

CALDECOTE TL141885 Population 63

The church is St. Mary Magdalene from the 13th century, unusual in having neither tower nor spire. Now declared redundant it has been converted into a private dwelling. To the north-west is Manor Farm and nearby fish ponds and spinneys. Between the ponds and Washingley Lane lies a Motte and Bailey earth and timber fortification, dating from Norman times. North of it is the site of the Medieval village of Washingley.

Footpaths to: Folksworth, Glatton, Lutton, Morborne, Washingley

CLOPTON TL067800 Population 95

A small hamlet of around 25 scattered dwellings some of which belong to the Ashton Estate, it has its own relatively modern parish church of St. Peter, consecrated in 1863 and built in late 13th century style. The tower is to the west and has a saddleback roof.

Clopton Manor House is neo-Jacobean and dated 1907. In the grounds are the remains of a previous Manor, late 17th century and home of the Dudley family. The gatehouse has coats of arms including the Dudley's. The Red Lion Inn and Motel offers a restaurant and accommodation.

That the road which passes through the village is so wide is due to the former siting of cruise missiles at Molesworth Airfield, two miles to the southeast, in the 1980's. Opened in 1941 it was first home for Australians flying Wellington bombers. It then became the Headquarters of the USAAF's 41st Combat Bombardment Wing and base for the 303rd Bombardment Group flying B-17's on 10,721 operational sorties over Europe. Except for a break between 1946 and 1951 the American Air Force has had the use of the site ever since which is currently in use as a military intelligence centre.

Footpaths to: Armston, Barnwell, The Giddings, Molesworth Airfield, Polebrook, Thurning, Titchmarsh, Winwick

GREAT GIDDING TL117832 Population 322

This peaceful village spans the fairly busy B660 road from the A1 to the north and the A14 to the south. It was founded in Anglo-Saxon times but was rebuilt in the mid 19th century after a disastrous fire. At sometime there were two concurrent Lords of the Manor which led to split allegiances.

The Parish Church is St. Michael's and was constructed from about 1250 to 1400. On the inside walls are stone carved shields with references to the Watson family, owners of the estate in the mid 1540's. It is set in a quiet graveyard some fifty yards from the road.

Baptist Chapel, Great Gidding

In Chapel End, and reached by footpaths from the main road and to the rear stands the Baptist Chapel dating from 1790. As is typical of such buildings it is of a plain box construction with galleries on wooden columns.

An important landmark is the disused and sail-less windmill now converted to a private dwelling. The local hostelry is the Fox and Hounds.

Footpaths to: Clopton, Little Gidding, Steeple Gidding, Sawtry, Winwick

HEMINGTON TL092850 Population 49

A tiny village on the Polebrook to Giddings road, the Parish Church is SS. Peter and Paul, with a Perpendicular west tower. The remainder is 1660 but gothicized in 1873. The stalls are thought to come from Fotheringhay College. There is a brass monument to Thomas Montagu who died in 1517. Next door is the Hemington Manor, possibly only part of an earlier, larger building. A number of the cottages belong to the Ashton estate.

Footpaths to: Thurning

LUDDINGTON-IN-THE-BROOK TL103837 Population 47

Literally named, it lies a few hundred yards inside the Northamptonshire boundary. First inhabited were workmen's cottages on the meadows each side of the Alconbury Brook and much damage was suffered from flooding until they were replaced by the landlord in 1863. On the wall of an old bakehouse is a Victorian postbox.

The church is the attractive St. Margaret's with a 13th century tower with clasping buttresses and the remains of a 15th century canopy. It was wisely built on a mound above flood level.

St. Margaret's Church, Luddington

Footpaths to: Barnwell, Polebrook, Thurning

LUTTON TL113878 Population 140

There has been Christian worship in the village, probably originally in a wooden structure, for 1200 years. The present church of St. Peter's has a Saxon cross-shaft c.800 AD and Norman carvings from the 12th century, relics of an earlier structure. Today's building has been reconstructed twice and has a 13th century chancel and north aisle; the south aisle is from the 14th and the tower and clerestory date from the 15th with renovation work done in the early twentieth century. There are monuments to the Apreece family.

As with other nearby villages such as Morborne, many of the more recent buildings are made of brick. One such is the Old Rectory which has been a private house since the parish was combined with Polebrook in 1924. The Manor House dating from the 1600s with later additions is made of the more usual limestone. Brook Farm House on the Polebrook Road is probably earlier. A recent "crop" to be seen occasionally in local fields are ostriches! Nearby (signposted) is Papley Farm where there are holiday cottages.

Footpaths to: Caldecote, Folksworth, Papley, Warmington

MORBORNE TL124913 Population 32

This village really lies beyond the boundary of our area, but a feature of it is that virtually all the buildings are in red brick. The small Parish Church of All Saints is reached via a drive shared with two cottages. On the wall of one is a Victorian postbox.

The Church has an unusual 17th century brick tower with stonework buttresses and capped with a dome of limestone slabs. The tower leans some 10" (25cm) from the vertical towrds the west. The chancel arch dates from the 12th century as does the priest's doorway and the next century saw the construction of the north and south arcades. East from the church is a round barrow.

The landmarks most prominent in the parish are the telecommunications and TV transmission masts to the west, just within our six-mile radius, which are lit at night by red warning lights. They lie about a mile from the Great North Road and three from the City of Peterborough.

Footpaths to: Caldecote, Folksworth, Haddon

POLEBROOK TL068871 Population 378

The church of All Saints was built from 1175 to 1250 and stands in the centre of the village. It is early English with Norman work, a broach spire and the interior benches may be Jacobean. The church was granted to Peterborough Abbey in the 1200s. There are two 14th century windows in the north transept and the nave roof is dated 1626.

Within is a roll of honour and the "stars and stripes" hang as a memorial to the men of the 351st Bomber Group USAAF, stationed at Polebrook Airfield from 1942 with Boeing B-17 Flying Fortresses. The station's complement was 2972 men and its aircraft flew 8600 sorties; 125 aircraft were lost.

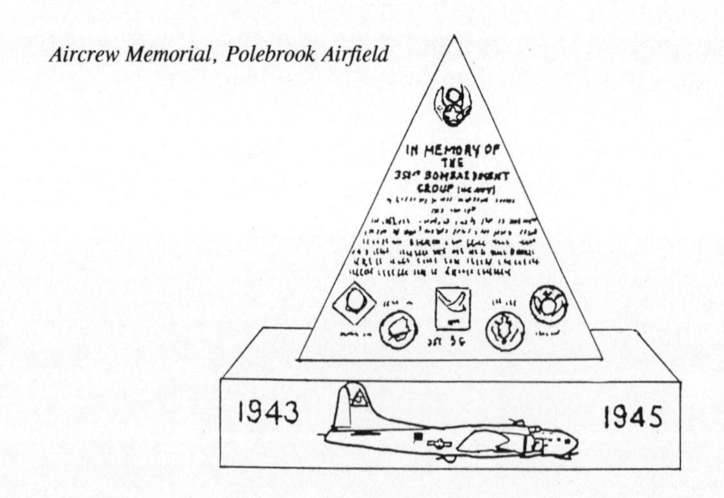

Aircrew Memorial, Polebrook Airfield

There are stone memorials at the east end of the disused runway which is signposted from the Polebrook to Lutton road. Clark Gable the actor served here as a commissioned air gunner and flew on several missions whilst making a film about air gunnery. [Note the memorial to James T. Stewart, Commanding Officer, is not about the film actor of that name, although he did fly with the Eighth Air Force].

From 1958 until 1963 when the airfield was closed Polebrook was used as a base for three Thor ballistic missiles, with two-megaton warheads, of 130 squadron RAF. These were part of Britain's first nuclear deterrent.

The parish includes the hamlets of Kingsthorpe and Armston. Many cottages are of local stone some with thatch roofs and some of Collyweston slate. Privately owned Polebrook Hall is Jacobean; the panelling in one room is dated 1626. It was extensively remodelled around 1719 including the provision of a staircase and iron gates to the east and the north. The posts for the gateway within the village are topped with statues.

In the village are the winter quarters for animals from a number of circuses. Elephants strolling in Main Street have been known! The local inn is the King's Arms.

Gates to Polebrook Hall

Footpaths to: Armston, Barnwell, Clopton, Kingsthorpe, Thurning

THURNING TL085828 Population 83

The church of St. John the Great lies at the centre of this small village and has a small stair tower capped by a conical roof giving access to the church roof in addition to a small spire. The chancel arch is Norman and later additions are 13th century. Drastic restoration took place in 1880 when the spired bell turret was added.

There is an equestrian centre nearby and buildings of note include a half-timbered cottage and a tithe barn, recently converted into a restaurant and shops.

St. John The Great, Thurning

Footpaths to: Polebrook, Hemington, Luddington, Molesworth Airfield, Polebrook

TITCHMARSH TL022798 Population 570

Originally an agricultural village standing on hills on the opposite side of the Nene Valley to Aldwincle, it can be easily identified at night by the illuminated pinnacled 15th century tower of St. Mary the Virgin standing 99ft. high. The Merchant Venturers of Bristol were at sometime involved in the establishment of the Church. A beacon was installed at the time of the Spanish Armada to warn of attack.

Twice within recent years the same corner pinnacle has been destroyed by lightning with structural damage in the village caused by flying masonry.

There is a fine window and Victorian wall-paintings in the building and a rare ha-ha serves as boundary to the west and south. Samuel Pepys visited in 1668. John Dryden, sometime Poet Laureate, spent his childhood here, possibly in the adjacent hamlet of Polopit and there is an epitaph to him in the church.

Colonel John Pickering, famous for his Regiment of Foot, one of Cromwell's original twelve, was born in the village and was educated in Oundle. The Pickering's were Lords of the substantial Manor of over 250 houses and cottages for two centuries. Their manor house has long gone and the family title became extinct in the mid 18th century although several monuments are in the church. The family had a private chamber (still visible but unfloored) over the porch.

To the south of the church and the green are the single storey 1756 Pickering Almshouses. There is a rectangular moat of a fortified manor house licensed in 1304 but ruined by 1363 to the south-west.

By the Nene is the old Titchmarsh mill on a Domesday site and now the base for the Upper Nene Sailing Club. Today's village has a mixture of four centuries' of buildings and is a popular dormitory for workers in Thrapston, Kettering, Corby and Peterborough. Public Houses are the Dog and Partridge and the Wheatsheaf. (See also Aldwincle for the Titchmarsh Nature Reserve).

Footpaths to: Aldwincle, Clopton, Keyston, Thorpe Waterville, Thrapston, Wigsthorpe

Combining the harvest

WARMINGTON TL078910 Population 753

One of the oldest known villages it was granted a charter in 660AD and continued to grow until the agricultural depression of 1874. It now serves mainly as a dormitory for workers in Oundle and Peterborough, though there are small holdings and farms around.

The old cottages were constructed from stone quarried at Barnack as was the broach spire of St. Mary the Virgin. The church was built between 1180-1220 and has a fine vaulted roof. Remodelling began before the end of the 13th century. The chancel was restored in 1865 and the nave in 1876. The font is dated 1662 and the pulpit is from the 15th century.

Warmington Manor House is Jacobean and was altered in 1677. The Red Lion pub on the "S" bend of the main road offers a place to rest awhile and the footpath to Fotheringhay skirts the property.

Footpaths to: Ashton, Elton, Fotheringhay

WINWICK TL104807 Population 97

Until 1960 the Elizabethan manor was the main employer in the village. It was home of the Mallory family and the first Lord was Sir Thomas, writer of Le Morte d'Arthur published by Caxton in 1470. Built of brick in the 16th century, it was altered in the 1920s and only about half the house is preserved. The gateway has four Roman Doric columns and is Elizabethan work.

The church of St. Michael and All Angels is 13th century with a Perpendicular tower and restoration included the chancel in the 19th century. It contains an old barrel organ. The church is set in an attractive aspect with the best views from the south.

Footpaths to: Clopton, The Giddings, Leighton Bromswold, Molesworth Airfield

APPENDIX A

THE RIVER NENE

Navigable from Northampton in the south to the Wash on the east coast it rises in the hills south of Daventry in the west of Northamptonshire. It provided the ideal route for invading Vikings evidence of whose occupation is found all along the river valley, particularly in village names .

There is a curiosity about this river. On old Ordnance Survey maps of the mid 19th century it is shown as the Nen. From the south to Thrapston it is still pronounced "Nen"; yet in much of our area it is called the "Neen".

The river meanders some 21 miles (35km) across the diameter of our circle of interest; its main tributaries are Harper's Brook joining at Aldwincle in the south and Willow Brook which flows into the main stream at Elton. Draining the hills to the east are the Barnwell, Polebrook, Warmington and Billing Brooks. To the south is Alconbury Brook and its tributaries.

At Titchmarsh Mill is a small marina and slipway with moorings; here too is the H.Q. of the Nene Cruising Club. Continuing downstream there are moorings at Wadenhoe. At the large Oundle Marina off the Barnwell Road is the H.Q. of the Oundle C.C. A private landing-stage is below the church at Tansor used by Oundle School canoeists. This was also the place where Viscount Montgomery of Alamein was taken out on the river by Oundle School boys during a visit in 1960.

Alongside the destroyed Fotheringhay Castle are more moorings. The Elton Boat Club has its H.Q. on a backwater at Warmington Mill although there are moorings at Elton itself. The Queens Head Inn at Nassington has its own and a slipway; you will need to book in advance. At Yarwell are moorings, a source of freshwater and facilities for sewage disposal.

Some features of the landscape like the bridge at Lilford or the two villages of Cotterstock and Tansor are extremely charming when seen from the river. Others, like the ten locks which gently lower the height from about 25 metres above sea level in the south to 15 metres a.m.s.l. at Yarwell, are less attractive but vital to waterborne traffic.

Loosely following the course of the river but also investigating some of its associated villages is the Nene Way, one of three Northamptonshire County Paths. (The others are Knightley Way and the Grafton Way) The total length of path covered in this book is just over 19 miles (32km).

APPENDIX B

BIBLIOGRAPHY

Buildings of England Series, Nikolaus Pevsner, (Penguin Books 1961)
Domesday Book Northamptonshire, (Phillimore 1979/1086)
8th Air Force Remembered, George Fox, (Iso Publications 1991)
Elton, Alan Clark, (Spiegl Press,1992)
English Place-Names, A.D. Mills, (Oxford, 1993)
Exploring Northamptonshire, Tony Noble, (Meridian Publications 1989)
Exploring the Nene Way, Mia Butler, (Countryside Books 1992)
History of the Oundle Schools, W.G.Walker, (Grocer's Company 1956)
Industrial Landscapes of the East Midlands, Palmer & Neaverson, (Phillimore, 1993)
Lutton's Church of St. Peter, Bert Saville, (Lutton PCC 1991)
Military Airfields 1939-45, Willis & Holliss (Enthusiasts Pub. 1990)
Moments of the Rose, Ian Addis, (Jema Publications 1994)
Mucky Lutton, Bert Saville, (Lutton PCC 1992)
Nature of Northamptonshire, NWT, (Barracuda 1989)
Nene Way, County Path Guide, (N.C.C. 1990)
Northamptonshire, Jack Gould, (Shire 1988)
Northamptonshire, Jon Stigner, (Alan Sutton 1994)
Northamptonshire Curiosities, Chris Billing, (Dovecote 1993)
Northamptonshire Past and Present Vol VIII, Northamptonshire Record Society 1990
Northamptonshire Rambles, Mia Butler, (Countryside Books 1991)

Northamptonshire Village Book, W. I., (Countryside Books 1989)
Oundle & The English Public School, Raymond Flowers, (Stacey Internat. 1989)
Oundle Town Guide and Trail, Oundle Town Council 1994
Pub Walks in Northamptonshire, Charles Whynne-Hammond, (Countryside Books 1993)
Some Ancient Interests of Fotheringhay, Parish Church
Titchmarsh Past and Present, Helen Belgion, (Marlow Durndell 1990)
Victorian Northamptonshire, Eric Jenkins, (Cordella Books 1993)
Wanderers in Northamptonshire 1 & 2, John & Vera Worledge, (Meridian Books 1992/94)
Waterside Walks Around Northamptonshire, Tony Noble, (Jema Publications 1992)

INDEX